For Phil
M.J.

For Mum and Dad,
Katy and Christopher,
and Mick and Keith
(for all their encouragement,
enthusiasm and countless
cups of tea over the years)
V.W.

First published 2007 by Walker Books Ltd, 87 Vauxhall Walk, London SE11 5HJ

This edition published 2008

1 3 5 7 9 10 8 6 4 2

Text © 2007 Martin Jenkins   Illustrations © 2007 Vicky White

The right of Martin Jenkins and Vicky White to be identified as author and illustrator respectively of this work
has been asserted by them in accordance with the Copyright, Designs and Patents Act 1988

This book has been typeset in Bulmer Display MT

Printed in China

British Library Cataloguing in Publication Data: a catalogue record for this book is available from the British Library

ISBN: 978-1-4063-1929-3

www.walker.co.uk

Ape

Martin Jenkins   illustrated by Vicky White

WALKER BOOKS
AND SUBSIDIARIES
LONDON • BOSTON • SYDNEY • AUCKLAND

There are five kinds of great ape in the world.
Each of them is different from the others ...
but not so very different. They're a family.

Four of them are very rare.
Orang-utan, Chimp, Bonobo, Gorilla.

Here they are...

Orang-utan

Orang-utan swings with her baby.
She has long hairy arms, with
strong hands for clutching at branches,
and feet that can grasp
the trunk of a tree.

That fruit's
out of reach ...

Orang-utans live in the rainforests of Borneo and
Sumatra in south-east Asia. They spend almost all their time in the trees.

11

... but not for long.

It's a durian.

Smelly, spiky,
delicious!

*Orang-utans are mostly vegetarian.
They eat a lot of different kinds of fruit
but are especially fond of durians.*

13

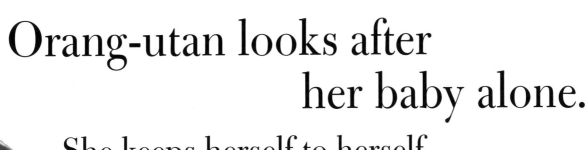

Orang-utan looks after her baby alone.

She keeps herself to herself,
high up in the treetops.

Each night she
builds a nest out of
branches to sleep on, then
pulls down a palm frond
to keep off the rain.

Chimp

Chimp lives in a gang

with his brothers and sisters
and uncles and cousins.

They squabble and play
and go roaming the hillsides,
hunting down monkeys
and digging up roots.

Chimpanzees
live in forests
and savannahs
in central and
west Africa.

Here's a termite nest.

Chimp pokes down a hole
with a long blade of grass,
then pulls out the grass
and licks off the termites.

Chimpanzees spend a lot of
time on the ground.
They eat lots of different things
and are very good at making
and using tools.

Chimp's gang sometimes
gets into fights with
other chimp gangs.

Nasty fights.
Lots of biting
and hitting.

23

Sometimes someone gets hurt.

Bonobo

Bonobo chatters and hoots,

calls to her friends,
while feasting on figs
high off the ground.

Bonobos live in the rainforest
of the Congo basin in central
Africa. They mostly eat
different kinds of fruit.

She drops from the tree and
moves quickly and quietly,
watching and listening –
there may be hunters
or leopards nearby.

Bonobos spend a lot of time
feeding in the trees
but often travel on
the ground from
one feeding place
to another.

31

Back in the treetops,
Bonobo plays with her friends,
safe again.

Gorilla

Gorilla lounges,

chewing on bamboo stems,

    chomping on leaves.

The silver hair on his back

    shows that he's old.

Gorillas live in the forests of central Africa. They can get to be forty or fifty years old.

Gorilla grunts
to his family,

then snoozes.

He wakes up, plays with his baby,
then snoozes some more.

Gorillas live in small family groups of one male with a few females
and their young. They are vegetarian and spend a lot of their time eating and sleeping.

He wakes up again,
chews on some bamboo,
builds a nest for the night and
turns in to sleep.

And the fifth kind of great ape is ...
do you know who?

You

... and me.

Us humans are part of the great ape family too.

We're not rare like the rest of them though –

there are lots and lots and lots of us.

But we do have other things in common.

We look like them (especially our faces).

We live long lives like them, and usually have only

one baby at a time, which takes years to grow up.

We're all clever too, probably cleverer

than any other animals.

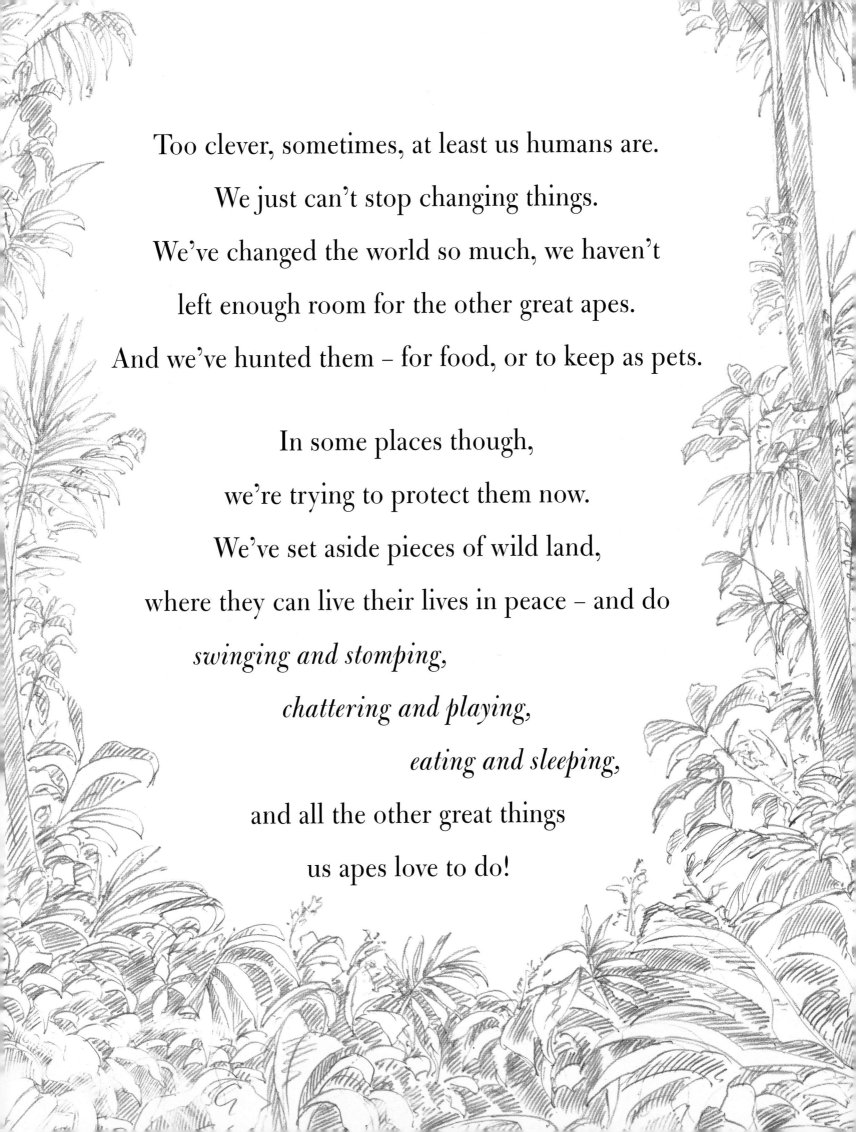

Too clever, sometimes, at least us humans are.

We just can't stop changing things.

We've changed the world so much, we haven't

left enough room for the other great apes.

And we've hunted them – for food, or to keep as pets.

In some places though,

we're trying to protect them now.

We've set aside pieces of wild land,

where they can live their lives in peace – and do

swinging and stomping,

chattering and playing,

eating and sleeping,

and all the other great things

us apes love to do!

Where the Great Apes Are

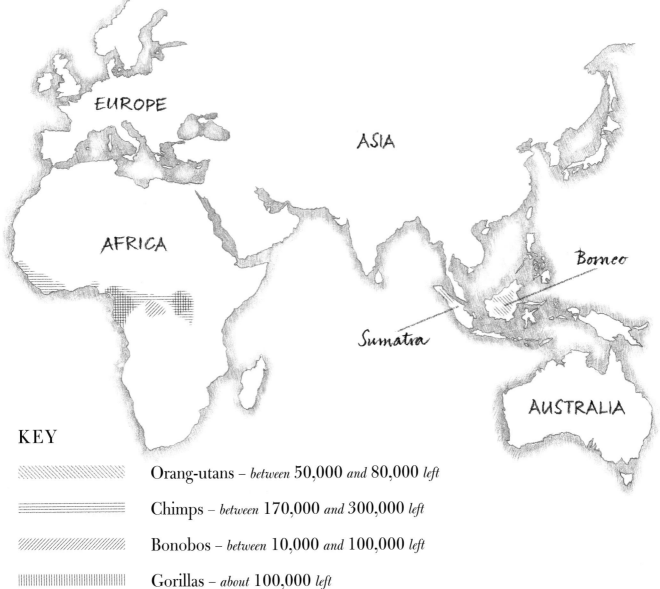

EUROPE

ASIA

AFRICA

Borneo

Sumatra

AUSTRALIA

KEY

Orang-utans – *between* 50,000 *and* 80,000 *left*

Chimps – *between* 170,000 *and* 300,000 *left*

Bonobos – *between* 10,000 *and* 100,000 *left*

Gorillas – *about* 100,000 *left*

The whole world   Humans – *more than* 6,000,000,000

These are the names and website addresses of some organisations trying to help conserve the great apes. (There are lots more.)

The Wildlife Conservation Society – www.wcs.org

The Worldwide Fund for Nature – www.wwf.org

Conservation International – www.conservation.org